# THE ARROWS OF THE ALMIGHTY

# The Arrows
## of the
## Almighty

A devotional study of
the character of Job

M. H. Finlay

**JOHN RITCHIE LTD**
CHRISTIAN PUBLICATIONS

40 Beansburn, Kilmarnock, Scotland

ISBN-13: 978 1 909803 66 4


Copyright © 2013 by John Ritchie Ltd.
40 Beansburn, Kilmarnock, Scotland


**www.ritchiechristianmedia.co.uk**

Typeset by John Ritchie Ltd., Kilmarnock
Printed by Bell & Bain Ltd., Glasgow

# *Contents*

# *Foreword*

SURELY THERE IS no child of God whose life is not touched at some point by the mystery of the permissive will of God. Its shadow falls upon all of us, and too often we "see not the bright light which is in the cloud." That those who seek to honor the name of God and to carry out His will should be led into depths of sorrow and suffering is a problem which has brought the "why" of bewilderment to countless lives. So truly is this a part of our mortal lives that it has pleased God, in giving His Word, to devote a whole book, that of Job, to the unfolding of His ways in our trials.

My dear friend, Mr. Finlay, has given us in these pages an acute analysis of Job's experiences and has shown that his trial was no arbitrary infliction but manifested the wise and gracious purpose of God to bless His servant with a richer revelation of Himself and a deeper sanctification of life. This is "the end of the Lord," the goal accomplished by the overruling of Him who is "very pitiful and of tender mercy."

If as we read these chapters we learn with Job and with many another to have "no confidence in the flesh" but rather to stand with contrite and humble spirit in the presence of God, the author's task will not have been in vain. We shall then prove how God delights to vindicate His trust in His servants and to bless them with the blessing that maketh rich, to which He adds no sorrow.

May it please the Lord to use these pages to the help and comfort of many hearts. I am sure that He will.

H. C. HEWLETT

author of *The Glories of our Lord* and *Companion of the Way*

# Introduction

THE BOOK OF JOB is considered by some scholars to be the oldest book in existence. If this is so, then God has performed a miracle of preservation in making this treasure available to us after the thousands of years of its history. A treasure it is most certainly, for it deals with the problem of sorrow and reveals the gracious purposes of an all-wise God who works out the sanctification of His own redeemed children through the refining processes of suffering.

So much of wonder and mystery is contained in this ancient writing that the reader finds difficulty in confining himself to any one line of study. In the lively debate between Job and his friends, such a variety of doctrines is touched upon that one is apt to become bewildered by the intricate pattern. In this present meditation, however, doctrinal issues are not particularly in view. Such a study is the work of scholars to whom, under God, we are deeply indebted. This little volume makes no claim to scholarship, being a devotional study of the character of Job, rather than a study of the Book of Job. A thorough study of this epic poem would require a knowledge of the original language so that the dramatic and literary form could be appreciated most fully, but to study the character of the man as revealed by his passionate outbursts is an exercise which may be undertaken prayerfully by any believer who finds in the experiences of Job a revelation of his own need and an exhibition of the gracious dealings of God, who desires, like the refiner of silver, to see the likeness of His own beloved Son produced in our lives.

At first Job is seen as a target for the "fiery darts of the wicked," but with the unfolding of God's purposes we are brought to realize that even the Enemy's "fiery darts" are transmuted by grace into "the arrows of the Almighty," painful without doubt, but effecting blessed results in the life of the godly patriarch.

Should some perplexed soul be enabled to see the rays of reflected glory shining from the life of Job as he maintained his integrity through the depths of his sorrows, then this simple study will have achieved its purpose. May it result in praise and thanks being given to God, the God of all grace.

# CHAPTER ONE

## A Perfect and an Upright Man

THERE WAS A MAN...whose name was Job." With these simple words we are introduced to one of the most impressive characters in the Bible. Our interest is aroused immediately by the glowing description given, not merely of his earthly prosperity but also of his deep piety and godliness. That he was a "success" in the eyes of men is clearly implied, but of much greater import is the declaration that his life was wellpleasing to God, who graciously records in this most ancient of all books the qualities which marked out Job as the most godly man of his day. Yes, he was that, for has not God recorded for all time His estimate of Job, that "there is none like him in the earth"? Truly a wonderful commendation!

To every sincere believer there is the ever present desire to please Him, and thus we may turn our attention reverently to this passage to learn what characteristics in Job merited this commendation. For, note well, it is not the praise of fallible men which is recorded but, in very truth, God's own appraisal and approval of this truly worthy man.

*"Hast thou considered my servant Job?"* (1:8). This question, addressed to Satan, indicates God's

11

great delight in His faithful servant and, indirectly, in all those who love and obey Him. This precious thought brings joy to our hearts, the more so when linked with the positive assurance in the words of Wisdom, "My delights were with the sons of men" (Prov. 8:31). The earnest believer is deeply conscious of weakness, failure, and sin as he toils along the rugged path in the steep ascent to Heaven, but when in His grace and wisdom God rolls back the veil of the unseen world, as in this verse, we learn that every longing for purity, for holiness—yea, for conformity to Christ—is exceedingly precious to the Father. In Numbers 23:21 we observe Israel of old, full of murmuring, discontent, carnality, and rebellion, provoking the Lord to anger daily, yet when Satan would curse and destroy them through Balak, King of Moab, Balaam is constrained to cry out, "He hath not beheld iniquity in Jacob, neither hath he seen perverseness in Israel. . . ." Thus it is with the children of God; sinful and worthless in themselves, they are nevertheless seen "in Christ" as clean every whit and the objects of the Father's love and care.

What though the Accuser roar of ills that I have done? I know them all, and thousands more; Jehovah findeth none!

Thus also, as Job diligently offered sacrifices on behalf of his family, desirous that nothing should be neglected that would honor God and secure the forgiveness of his household, he little knew that just beyond the limit of frail human knowledge Jehovah, the God of grace and faithfulness, was actually holding him up as a pattern of godliness, even to the extent of suggesting that Satan should focus all his attention upon him.

"Have you considered my servant Job?" asks Jehovah. "Have you observed the singular purity of his life and motives? There indeed is a man—a son of Adam's fallen race, 'tis true, yet one who in his faith and obedience to My will, is above all your subtleties, a man whose delight is in the law of the Lord. Consider him!"

Oh, we ask ourselves, is such a thing possible? Yes, assuredly, though not until we reach Immanuel's Land shall we fully understand the joy and satisfaction that God finds in the devotion of His Own redeemed ones. Yet an inkling of this is disclosed in those unfathomable words of Paul, "That ye may know what is...the riches of the glory of *his inheritance in the saints*" (Eph. 1:18).

"*There is none like him in the earth.*" This phrase can mean nothing less than what it says, that God, who knows the hearts of all men, God before whom all secrets are laid bare, states plainly that Job was without a peer among the sons of men.

"*Perfect.*" Subsequent events in Job's history make it plain that he was not perfect in the sense of being a sinless man. He was not sinless but he was sincere. Job was just as good to the eye of God as he was to the fallible scrutiny of his fellowmen. There was no conscious hypocrisy in his life.

"*Upright.*" His life before men was blameless. In his outward walk before friends and neighbors there was nothing that could bring reproach upon the name of his God. There was no just cause for censure from man or devil.

"*One that feareth God.*" There was true reverence,

fear in the Old Testament sense, as Job stood before God. There was true appreciation of God's impeccable holiness, His awful majesty and unapproachable glory, and thus Job walked humbly before his God in an attitude of willing obedience to the revealed will of God.

"*And escheweth evil.*" His knowledge of the holy will of God was sufficient to give unerring direction to his life. His God hated sin, therefore Job abhorred it also, and "abstained from all appearance of evil."

\*        \*        \*

In less than thirty words, Jehovah thus depicts the *character* of a man who pleased Him well. Moreover, from the divine record of his *practices,* we obtain further glimpses of the way in which Job's piety was expressed.

*He was a faithful parent* (1:5). In patriarchal days, the father was the family priest, and Job followed faithfully in this divine order, teaching his family God's will, and in faith and humility offering sacrifices continually with the single motive that his children might learn to love and serve Jehovah. The family altar was maintained.

*He was wholly at rest in the will of God* (1:21). When, without warning, his peaceful existence was disrupted so violently and all his dearest and best was swept away in a sudden torrent of satanic fury, Job retained his spiritual balance; he worshiped God, saying, "The LORD gave and the LORD hath taken away. Blessed be the name of the LORD."

Thus far we have discovered a man beloved of the Lord, a godly man, a man delighting in and dwelling in the will of God. To our consternation we see this peerless man now plunged without warning into unfathomable depths of sorrow, suffering, and despair by the greatest accumulation of diabolical torments and miseries that our minds could imagine. To Job himself, the agonies were so great that they distorted his mental and spiritual vision. But we, from our detached point of view, are privileged to discover the purpose of his sorrows, plainly portrayed in the Scriptures for our edification.

Thus we may analyze reverently the processes of his trials and observe his reactions, the reactions of his friends also and, finally, the divine answer, that we might gain a fuller understanding of the tremendously important truth of sanctification exemplified in the life of Job as the outcome of his awful experiences.

# CHAPTER TWO

# The Factors Involved in the Trial of Job

THE DISASTERS which overtook Job were multiple. In order to estimate the severity of each blow, we must endeavor with the guidance of the Holy Spirit to evaluate the varied factors which produced a cumulative weight that crushed him to the earth, a broken man.

The prime factor, the author, and instigator of all that fell upon Job was none less than Satan himself. This is not surmise; it is plainly stated in this portion of God's Holy Word. Job had not wronged Satan, and yet we see all the malice of the Devil directed toward the patriarch for the simple reason that Job's life was lived to the glory of God. It is fashionable today to reject belief in the existence of a personal devil, but in this ancient book God has revealed not merely the existence of Satan and his power and privileges but also the venomous malignity and contempt with which he regards those who seek to honor and obey the God against whom he himself has rebelled. Thus it is patent that for any son of Adam's race to declare loyalty to God and to His Word is to incur all the virulent hatred of this cunning and relentless foe.

Satan is introduced into the story as he enters brazenly into the presence of God. Elsewhere he is termed "the accuser of the brethren," and without doubt his approach to the throne of glory was to launch an attack against some of the saints of the Most High. However, God, the omniscient One, anticipates Satan's base intention. Before the subtle tongue of the Adversary could bring a charge, the Lord deprived him of the initiative by challenging him with the simple question, "Hast thou considered my servant Job?" Satan, you accuser, you slanderer, you father of lies, have you observed that faithful man? God knew that Satan had paid more than usual attention to the godly patriarch and knew that there was especially violent hatred against him because every satanic attempt to seduce him had ended in utter failure.

Satan's reply was tacitly an admission of defeat. He had no charge to lay, nothing at all. The godliness of Job was a fact that could not be challenged or gainsaid by man or demon, but Satan had in his quiver one fiery dart, which he used with telling effect.

"Oh, yes, Job is good," he sneers, "but there is a reason for *that*. DOES JOB FEAR GOD FOR NOUGHT? Is not all his vaunted piety inspired by the base motive of self-interest? It *pays* him to be good! Hast not Thou made an hedge about him, and about all his house, and about all that he hath *on every side?*" (1:10).

Seldom indeed would one desire to choose the words of Satan as a text upon which to base a message to believers, but surely we are justified in giving attention to this surprising admission. The mighty ruler of principalities and powers of the darkness of this world admits that he is powerless to touch Job.

God has built a hedge, a wall of complete protection around him so that the Devil searches in vain for a vulnerable point at which to launch an attack. How our timid hearts should leap for joy to see our Archenemy baffled, defeated, and impotent, unable to destroy the faith and piety of a fallible mortal around whom God has built a wall of protecting grace! Surely this was the thought in the mind of the writer of the Book of Proverbs as he wrote, "The name of the LORD is a strong tower: the righteous runneth into it, and is safe." So also Israel proved Jehovah to be a wall of fire by night and by day a pillar of cloud, through which the Egyptians could not pass. Whereas Satan cannot "break in," it is possible for the believer by willfulness to "break out" and thus emerge from the shelter of that hedge of divine grace. "Whoso breaketh an hedge, a serpent shall bite him," declares the Preacher (Eccles. 10:8). And no wonder! The hedge is to keep Satan out. The child of God who through willfulness or foolishness "breaks out" of the hedge thereby places himself in the sphere of the activity of that "old serpent, called the Devil," who will most assuredly "bite him," for under such circumstances there is no promise of divine protection.

And so we return to the picture of the tempter, unable to reach Job within the safety of the "hedge" and pouring out his venom in the base insinuation that Job was good because of ulterior motives. To God Satan says, "You have protected him; you have blessed the work of his hands; he enjoys popularity, wealth and comfort. But allow me to get through that impregnable hedge; let me but touch him, and he will rise and curse you to your face!"

That was the challenge! Satan had succeeded in the presence of the "sons of God," before the very throne of glory, in laying a charge that sought to dishonor God and discredit His servant Job. Let us not minimize the seriousness of the charge. God had declared that Job was without an equal in the earth. If then Satan could prove his assertion, he would demonstrate that no mortal man could be sincerely and disinterestedly loyal to God. What could be done to counter this dastardly accusation? There was one way, one only!

God knew Job. Knowing that he could pass the test, the *only way* for God to vindicate His beloved servant was to remove the "hedge" which was the basis of the diabolical insinuation. Therefore God granted to Satan the power to deprive Job of everything conducive to selfish pleasure and natural satisfaction. With hellish glee, the Adversary hastened from the presence of God, fully confident that he would now demonstrate the truth of his charge and expose the hypocrisy of the man who would be in his baleful power without recourse to that wall of protecting grace.

As we know, Job remained true to God. When Satan re-enters the presence of God in the second phase of the trial, he makes no admission of defeat. He merely propounds a new theory. Job is callous! He is insensitive to material losses or even family tragedies. "But," says Satan, "touch *him*—touch his body, and see how quickly he will succumb to temptation."

To this final demand for power to lay his hands upon Job himself, God accedes. He grants His permission for Satan to do his very utmost. It is only by trial to the absolute limit that Job can be vindicated.

Even though Satan had received permission to test Job to the end, we must not for one moment imagine that Job was forsaken in his time of great need. We find assurance on this point in a little-known portion of Scripture in the prophecy of Zechariah, chapter one. There we read of a similar scene but one with a very different background. The prophet sees a vision of mysterious riders upon horses and in response to his request to know the meaning of the vision, God once more draws back the veil of the unseen realm as the reply is given by the angel, "These are they whom the Lord hath sent to walk to and fro through the earth" (Zech. 1:10).

How full of consolation for God's people is a statement like this! Satan, when appearing as the accuser of Job in the presence of God, said that he came "from going to and fro in the earth and from walking up and down in it." And what the aim and object of his restless activity in the earth is, we are told by the Apostle Peter in his earnest warning, "Be sober, be watchful, for your adversary the devil (full of hatred and fiendish cunning, as his names imply, and ever ready with fresh traps and snares for our destruction)—as a roaring lion, walketh about seeking whom he may devour." If left to ourselves and his devices for one day, where should we be? But, blessed be God, "The Angel of Jehovah encampeth (as with a great invisible host) round about them that fear Him, and delivereth them"; and if there are evil, malignant spirits (ever restlessly walking to and fro in the whole earth on their mischievous intent of hindering, if they cannot frustrate, the gracious purposes of God, and the manifestation of His Kingdom on earth), God also has *His* messengers who walk to and fro to counteract and frustrate Satan's designs, and to succour and shield, and in many more ways than we know, to be ministering spirits to them who shall be heirs of salvation. (David Baron, *The Visions and Prophecies of Zechariah*)

From this we realize that guardian angels are not mythical but real beings, to whose ministry we owe much, though we are not fully aware of their presence and activity. Thus we can rest assured that when the "hedge" around Job was removed, the angelic hosts were unseen but real witnesses of all that took place.

But even more precious to us than hosts of guardian angels is the word of our Lord and Master Himself, spoken under apparently similar circumstances, to Peter, "Simon, Simon, behold, Satan hath desired to have you, that he may sift you as wheat: but *I have prayed for thee,* that thy faith fail not" (Luke 22:31-32). The Lord did not say, "Fear not, Satan cannot touch you." Rather He inferred that Satan would be permitted to do his worst, but that all the concentrated malice of the enemy could not succeed in destroying the faith of even Peter. Why? His security—and ours—is expressed in those words to Peter, "I have prayed for thee." Is that not better than guardian angels, ministering spirits? We have a great High Priest, greater than angels and made higher than the heavens, who ever liveth to make intercession for us (Heb. 7:25-26).

No, with such a God watching in His sovereign power, Job was not abandoned, even though he may have thought that such was the case. Thus encouraged, we return to our observation of the "sifting" of Job, in the process of which a masterly array of active agents and inanimate factors was employed, aimed at the destruction of Job's testimony and his trust in the faithfulness of God. With devastating effect, Satan made use of:

1. *The Sabeans and the Chaldeans.* To a man of the world, the depredations of these enemies could be dismissed simply as "the fortunes of war." Savage bands of marauders stole upon Job's servants, who were peacefully engaged in pastoral and agricultural pursuits. In a sudden brutal attack, the servants were massacred, and the oxen, asses, and camels taken away. The oxen, asses, and camels provided the "horsepower" for the tilling of Job's broad acres and, together with the skilled servants, represented to a large extent his means of gaining wealth. In one stroke all was lost. But as the solitary survivor blurted out his tragic news, Job, being a just and godly master, was concerned with more than loss of his wealth. Those servants were loved and trusted members of his household. Job could not know that this sudden, grievous loss was anything more than a casual raid. He had no means of knowing that it was but the first cruel episode in a process that was to leave him stripped and broken. We from our vantage point know what lay behind it, and we do well to ponder the ubiquity of Satan's influence in that he could induce in the Sabeans and Chaldeans a greedy desire to seize Job's property at the psychological moment, causing one group to converge (in three bands) upon the camels, while from another locality the Sabeans appear to pounce on the asses and oxen.

2. *The forces of nature.* This paragraph brings us deeper into the mysterious realm of Satan's power.

Scripture calls him "the prince of the power of the air." That this is no empty language is clear from his ability to control the elements. To Job, deeply grieved and perplexed over the tragic loss of his servants, oxen, asses, and camels, comes a gasping terror-stricken messenger who delivers news of another devastating blow, far more subtle and perplexing to Job than the first.

"The fire of God—" gasps the man, "the fire of God has fallen from heaven and has consumed the sheep and the shepherds! All are gone; I only am left!" The first blow came from raiding marauders, common enough in those far-off days, but that his sheep and their attendants should be destroyed by what we term an "act of God" was a baffling mystery. Did Satan prompt the messenger to use unwittingly those words, "the fire of God," to deepen the mental distress of Job? Those flocks of sheep were more than symbols of pastoral wealth. From the flocks, the firstlings, the finest and the best were dedicated to God. The regular sacrifices for Job and his household, sacrifices ordained by Jehovah to cover the sins of his family, were chosen from those flocks.

Was it possible that his offerings were no longer acceptable to God? Had not the "fire of God" destroyed the lambs which were the only means by which he could approach a holy God? Since in those patriarchal days material prosperity and security were accepted as an indication of God's favor, this destruction would make a deeper impression on Job than it would in our modern complex world where disasters of our own making fill the columns of our daily newspapers.

But even as Job sat there pondering the problem, another man was running with the most grievous news of that whole tragic day. "Master, master, your sons and your daughters—" How Job's heart would miss a beat! "Your sons and daughters were feasting and a great wind smote the house. All are dead, even the servants, and I alone escaped to tell you!"

As this crushing news was brought home to his dazed senses, it must have confirmed the thoughts aroused by the loss of his flocks. What secret sins had been indulged in by his children that God should destroy them? Had all his prayers, the family worship, the constant sacrifices, and the patient instruction in the ways of God been in vain—futile to avert the judgment of God? Was it possible God had not accepted his offerings and had refused to pardon the young people? This must have broken Job's heart. He had apparently failed so seriously in his duty as father and family priest that Jehovah had cut off his children!

That this was Job's initial thought and final conclusion is obvious from his immediate reaction. Giving full vent to his grief with suitable outward expresson of the depth of his anguish, Job falls down before God in the attitude of worship and exclaims, "The LORD gave, and the LORD hath taken away; blessed be the name of the LORD." There is not the slightest suggestion in his words or attitude that Job attributed his loss to any other source but the hand of God.

3. *Ill health.* As we enter a consideration of this phase of the trial, we are compelled to realize the implacable cruelty of Satan's merciless hostility. Still unsatisfied by the spectacle of the broken-hearted

patriarch lying in dust and ashes, he now touches Job's body, causing loathsome and excruciating boils to break out and to add physical torment to his mental distress. While we retain the buoyancy of glowing health, it is comparatively easy to maintain a brave attitude to the vicissitudes of life, but when we are plunged into the dark vale of sickness, weakness, and suffering, how suddenly our vision is bedimmed and our perspective distorted! If ever a man was in danger of being engulfed in the Slough of Despond, surely that man was Job!

And yet more was to follow. His physical pain was intense, but there was to be added an increasing load of mental agony, and surely suffering of the mind is more unbearable than that of the body!

4. *His wife's attitude* (2:9). Various opinions have been expressed on the motive which prompted Job's wife to speak as she did. Some suggest that she was not his equal in faith and spiritual understanding and was urging him to give up his religious profession as worthless, as if to say, "Deny your God and die. Let go your belief in the future life, and close your eyes upon the sorrows of this life. Die, and be at peace in the grave!"

Others suggest that her love and concern for Job were so great that in effect she was saying, "I cannot bear to see you suffer so; better to curse God and die—be cut off!" We offer no comment as to her motive, for whatever her reasons may have been in speaking as she did, there is no doubt as to the effect it produced upon her husband (2:10; 19:17). It is plain that the loss of his wife's companionship and fellowship in faith was a cruel and unexpected addition to his sufferings.

5. *His friends*. His friends were kind. They came to him at once; they sat down with him and entered into the outward expressions of sympathy which were in full accord with the customs of the day. How he must have valued their considerate, silent sympathy during those seven days of excruciating pain and grief! But when they began to speak, being only fallible men, they spoke harshly. Sound advice they sometimes gave, but it was given without due consideration for the state of their friend and only deepened his mental anguish, contributing nothing to his need for consolation. Was not even this a barb added to the fiery darts of the Wicked One, as Job points out in his pathetic words in 6:14-27? In this paragraph, he describes his feelings by the use of a very expressive metaphor. As a band of travelers through the desert look with intensity for water, so he longed for comfort. The traveler who has passed through the desert in winter has seen the gushing streams fed by the ice and snow. Now, tormented by thirst, he presses on to the watercourse, only to find that it has dried up in the heat of summer. So Job said, "I expected to find comfort from you, if from no other source, but you have disappointed me just like a brook that has become dry in a time of most desperate need." The same poignant truth is expressed in the words of David, "For it was not an enemy that reproached me; then I could have borne it:...but it was thou, a man mine equal, my guide and mine acquaintance" (Ps. 55:12-13).

6. *His servants* (19:16). Some, at least, of his servants were spared when so many perished. How strange is the attitude of these survivors! Gone is their deference for the greatest man of the East, gone

is their willing service and prompt obedience as, stripped of all earthly supports, their master sits on the ash heap, weeping and groaning. No doubt he had cared for these servants and had comforted them in many a trial, but now they added to his sense of loss by showing him only contempt.

7. *The mockers.* Job makes frequent reference to these "mockers," who were possibly ungodly neighbors whose impious lives had been rebuked by the godliness and morality of Job. Evidently they gloated and rejoiced over his sudden and complete downfall. How grievous it is for a good man to endure the vile slanders and malicious mockings of evil neighbors! Job, ever mindful of the glory of God, would realize that although the taunts were aimed at him they also brought reproach on the name of the Lord. Godless men are ever ready to say, "He trusted in God; let him deliver him now," as they said of our blessed Saviour in the hour of His agony. The mockers doubtless made capital out of the fact that God had obviously failed to protect one whose life was devoted to His service. "Many there be which say of my soul, There is no help for him in God" (Ps. 3:2).

\*        \*        \*

In drawing this section to a close, we do well to take note of Job's own dramatic summary of his state and of his personal feelings while passing through the crushing experiences outlined above. In 19:6-20 he likens himself to the following:

1. A man taken in a net, without hope of escape (v. 6).
2. A man in a court of law, pleading for justice but not given a hearing (v. 7).

3. A wanderer, lost in byways in deep darkness (v. 8).
4. A king, dethroned and humiliated (v. 9).
5. A tree, stripped, felled, and destroyed (v. 10).
6. A city, besieged by strong enemies (vv. 11-12).
7. A lonely outcast (vv. 13-14).
8. A despised foreigner, even in his own house (v. 15).
9. A master, insulted and ignored by his slaves (v. 16).
10. A man who has lost his wife's affection, mocked by little children, abhorred by his dearest friends, and tormented by loathsome disease (vv. 17-20).

To such a state the greatest of all the men of the East was reduced as Satan attempted to discredit the character and piety of Job.

Thus far we have noted some of the agents which were used by Satan for the accomplishment of his diabolical purpose, and the story would be unrelieved blackness but for one all-important feature. God was, to borrow a poetic phrase, "standing in the shadows" watching. How we should praise Him for this clear revelation in the history of Job! Were it true that Satan could use human beings and forces of nature and disease to attack and destroy any man who incurred his wrath, well might we, as do the heathen, attempt to placate and propitiate this being, malignant, powerful, and mysterious. But we have the more sure Word of God. Light shines through the gloom as we learn that there *was* another agent at work. This agent was Jehovah, who had permitted the Devil to break through the hedge of divine protection. Behind every fiery dart, every brutal blow, behind the accumulation of sorrow and pain, was the unseen but ever-present God who knew that the process of crushing would issue only in a greater spiritual development and a life of more positive sanctification in His beloved servant.

# CHAPTER THREE

# Glimpses of Job's True Faith

HAVING GAINED SOME INSIGHT into the sorrows of Job, we desire now to see another aspect of the same experience, a brighter side. Like stars shining in midnight blackness, we find glimpses of Job's true faith appearing through the horror of his grief and pain. Job was a godly man. He was also a man of great faith, able to stand all the tests that Satan devised to destroy him. It is not surprising then that ever and anon throughout his long and impassioned discourses we find glorious bursts of triumphant certainty which demonstrate his unshakable faith in his God. He could still trust, though he could not understand! To list some of these precious outbursts will prove a profitable study for us. We observe:

1. *His unhesitating acceptance of the will of God* (1:20-21). This point has been noted already, but we do well to restate here that when his little world came crashing down around him he humbly accepted the disasters as the will of God. To Job God's will was "good and acceptable and perfect" (Rom. 12:1).

2. *His deep knowledge of God* (9:2-15). He could accept the will of God because he *knew* God! Some idea of Job's knowledge of God may be gained by observing the manner in which he used the divine titles.

30

*a. God (Elohim).* This title occurs on the lips of
Job in 1:5 and in many subsequent passages in the
book. This name is used 2550 times in the Old
Testament, beginning with the opening verses of
Genesis. We learn that this name contains the
meaning of the Creator, the one eternal God to
whom all power belongs. Dr. Campbell Morgan
says, "It refers to absolute, unqualified, unlimited
energy."

*b.* LORD *(Jehovah).* The most familiar of all scrip-
tural titles, the name Jehovah occurs in the He-
brew scriptures about 6823 times. The meaning
was given to Moses by God Himself in Exodus
3:14 as "I am that I am." Explained thus, it directs
our attention to a God who is the ever-living One,
unchanging through the ages, the fount of life.
Jehovah was the name by which God chose to
reveal Himself as the personal God and Saviour
of the despised and persecuted Hebrews, the name
by which He pledged Himself to effect their deliverance from Egyptian bondage and to bear them
safely to the land of promise and blessing. Thus
we know Jehovah as the God of all grace and
infinite compassion, ever living, ever present, and
unchangeable. The words of Job take on new
values as he cries out in his distress, "Jehovah
gave and Jehovah hath taken away...." It was
his loving, compassionate LORD, the covenant-
keeping God, whom he accepts as the Author of
his grief, though why it should be so, his perplexed and tortured mind cannot understand.

*c. The Almighty (El Shaddai)* (6:4; 23:16;
27:2). There is diversity of opinion among
scholars as to the exact meaning of this title, but

most are agreed that it conveys the thought of the love and tender care of the One who is all-sufficient; the mighty One of resource who "daily loadeth us with benefits." Like a father, *El Shaddai* pities His children who, in their weakness and utter dependence, may derive their needed supplies of sustenance and daily grace from His loving bounty.

Out of the 48 occurrences of the name in the Old Testament, 31 are found in the Book of Job. The fact is arresting. It is not just that the writer of Job was fond of this name of God; the Holy Spirit, the Author of the entire Scripture, designed it so. For no Old Testament book more wonderfully reveals the mighty, tender love of God for His child than Job does. The keenest part of the travail of Job was the thought—so bluntly and cruelly stated by his friends—that the *Almighty* had stricken him! If *such* a God were chastening him so sorely, they inferred, Job must be wicked indeed. The anguish of Job lay in the fact that he knew his own integrity, and could not understand why the God whom he loved and trusted should deal with him so. He had sought sincerely to worship and serve El-Shaddai—yet this calamity had happened to him. But because he truly knew Him to be *El Shaddai*, and despite the taunts of his accusers, he held on to the truth concerning the character of God as he had come to know Him, and was able to rise above his anguish to the sublime height of faith in the declaration, "Though He slay me, yet will I trust in Him."—H. F. Stevenson.

"For the arrows of *the Almighty* are within me, the poison whereof drinketh up my spirit" (6:4). "He hath...set me up for his mark. His archers

compass me round about,. . ." (16:12-13). Job's
tortured mind expressed its distress in this striking
metaphor, a figure of speech also used by David
(Ps. 38:2) and Jeremiah (Lam. 3:12-13).
Around his defenseless body, it seemed, were the
"archers," shooting into him as into a target "the
arrows of the Almighty," poisoned barbs which
seemed likely to destroy him. Instead of destroying
him, however, "the arrows of the Almighty"
brought to him a new realization of his own need
of the ministry of the Great Physician.

d. *The Holy One* (6:10). This is a descriptive title
which presents to our minds One who is the pure
source of all perfection, the very fount of unsullied,
unchanging righteousness, in whom there is no
variableness nor shadow of turning. Job pleads his
sincerity in handling the word of the Holy One
and thus he knows that, baffling though the thought
may be, all God's ways must be right. The Holy
One could not do wrong.

e. *The Preserver of Men* (7:20). In the use of
this ascription Job plainly admits his conviction
that his life and health, his material comforts—yea,
his all—are in the hand of God; therefore his sorrows could not be the result of chance.

f. *Lord (Adonai)* (28:28). This title, which is
used 340 times in the Old Testament, means simply
"Master." Job implies his ready submission to
the will of his absolute Master in the words, "The
fear of the Lord [*Adonai*], that is wisdom." The
truly wise man is he who submits gladly, with
reverent fear, to his divine Lord and Master. The
attitude of the slave to his master is that of immediate and sustained submission, with unques-

tioning obedience. Why then should Job question
the ways of his Master?

*     *     *

Thus we see that Job had more than a basic belief
in the existence of God. Secular writers would attempt to persuade us that in ages past men had only
an elementary religion of idols and spirits, but Job
knew his God by a variety of names which expressed
the character and attributes of the eternal Father
in a real and intimate way. This thought of intimacy
is further expressed in the words, "Whom I shall see
for myself,...and *not a stranger*" (19:27, margin).

Moreover, Job gives a graphic description of the
ways of God in passages like 9:4-14.

To continue our observation of Job's faith, we note:

3. *His confession of human frailty* (9:11-12; 9:30-
31). No false pride kept him from an open confession of his own sinfulness and weakness in the presence of a holy God.

4. *His longing for an adequate mediator* (9:32-
35). Speaking from his own experience, he says feel-
ingly, "He is not man." Job knew that he could not,
dare not, approach a holy God without a "daysman,"
an accredited mediator. His reason, his conscience,
and his knowledge of God all combined to impress
upon him the necessity of having "an advocate with
God," but in his distress he knew not where to find
Him. With reverence and humility (for it is not because of any merit in us) we should praise God for
the light of the sacred page which reveals to us that
not only do we need the Mediator of whom Job
spoke but that He has come, the virgin-born God-
Man, who has laid His hand upon both God and man
(I Timothy 2:5; I John 2:1).

5. *His triumphant faith* (13:15, 18). Job's knowledge of God, though incomplete and defective, so inspired him in his anguish that he rose above the limitations of his sorely tried body and shouted, "Though he slay me, yet will I trust in him." Yes, let the hand of God be upon me in all the severity of His chastening and still I would rather be in that hand than anywhere else in God's creation. Faith then adds, "I know that I shall be justified. The God whom I know and have served for so long is not One who will leave my cry unheard and unanswered. I know not how, but I believe that my God can be just and yet be the justifier of the ungodly." (See Rom. 3:26; 4:5.)

Then, as his faith lifts his soul above the sordid environment of the dust heap, he cries out, "I *know* that my redeemer liveth..." (19:25). "I *know* that Adam was restored to favor; I *know* that Abel was accepted; I *know* that Enoch pleased God; I *know* that Noah was delivered from the universal judgment; I *know* that the blood of my sacrifices speaks for me before God's throne; I *know* whom I have believed, and He cannot lie; He has promised a Redeemer, and though I may not know the time nor the method of His coming, HE LIVES and shall stand upon the earth!"

Is not his triumphant faith? Is not this the feature of the lives of those saints of old of whom God has recorded, "These all died in faith, not having received the promises..."?

A further glimpse of his triumphant faith appears in the familiar words which have cheered and sustained many a burdened, trembling saint following along the pathway of discipline. "He knoweth the way that I take; when he hath tried me, I shall come forth as gold" (23:10). "Ah," says Job, "He knoweth —I do not yet know!"

> Dear Lord, I cannot see where Thou art leading me!
> I cannot tell if thorns or roses strew the way;
> My future is concealed; Thou hast not yet revealed
> Thy will in me, nor do I for the knowledge pray.
>
> What streams I have to cross, of sorrow, pain or loss,
> Are not for me to fear—I shall not be dismayed:
> Content if Thou, my Guide, art ever near my side,
> That I may hear Thee whisper, "Child, be not afraid."

Job saw his sorrows not as a judgment but as a refining process! And he was right; God later confirmed this. "Out of these crushing sorrows," cries Job, "I shall come forth as gold, refined, purified."

Gold is tried by fire to purify it. Alloyed and impure gold loses its true luster and is hard, unyielding, unusable. But the refining fire purifies it, restores its true golden beauty and renders it malleable and useful for every precious work. As we observe the necessity of the fire and the refining process, we learn also in Scripture that when God would use gold it must be pure gold, and then He requires that it be subjected to a further process. He asks for "beaten gold." The cherubim of glory over the mercy seat were to be made of pure gold, beaten (Exod. 25:18). The candlestick was of beaten gold (Num. 8:4). Before the holy place could be illuminated by the glowing lamps of that seven-branched lampstand, the gold had to be beaten. Does not that suggest to us that if any earth-born material is to be used to the fullest extent for God's glory, there must be both the refining process and the beating process? (Even the incense had to be beaten very small!) When the high priest went into the holy place in his service for God, he wore a garment into which were woven golden "wires," produced by beating gold into very thin plates (Exod. 39:3).

It is said that pure gold can be beaten into plates not more than one-hundred-and-fifty-thousandth of an inch in thickness. No wonder then, that gold beaten until it is very thin is a fitting symbol of the believer under the refining processes of trials. Our God, in His infinite wisdom and love, knows just how much of the refining furnace and the beating we can stand; knows that we may be beaten so thin and yet not destroyed in the process, from which we emerge in the condition that will bring us to the utmost usefulness. As a result our God will receive the glory which is His due.

We learn another interesting point from Sir William Bragg, who says, "It is very curious that when this beaten gold has been heated to a dull red, it becomes permanently transparent and white by reflected light." The fiery trial is not to produce a mere transient improvement, but it stamps us with an eternal quality; the effect is permanent! This thought sheds a blaze of light on the verse, Revelation 21:18, which states: "And the city was pure gold, like unto clear glass." Permanently transparent! Surely this pictures the saints of earth, redeemed by the blood of the Lamb, shining forth in the kingdom of their Father, purified and radiant from the effect of the refining and beating processes and glowing throughout eternity, with the glory of "pure gold, like unto clear glass," reflecting the dazzling whiteness of the rays of the Sun of Righteousness.

In our saner moments, would we ever dream of asking our heavenly Father to cease His process of refining, when the fire and the beating must result, as Job affirms bravely, in our coming forth as gold? We owe a tremendous debt of gratitude to Job for this glorious and sustaining message from the heat of the furnace. Yea, rather let us praise Him who permitted His servant to pass through that pathway of suffering in order to display the heights to which true faith may rise under trials, and the ultimate and eternal outcome of such trials.

6. *Job admits no second causes.* "Who knoweth not in all these that the hand of the LORD *hath wrought this?*" (12:9). "Know now that *God hath overthrown me...*" (19:6). "The hand of *God hath touched me*" (19:21).

How could Job say this? What of the Sabeans and the Chaldeans? What of the cruelty of neighbors and friends? Job evidently considers them to be merely incidental to the fact of the sovereignty of God when he says, "The hand of the LORD hath wrought this." Is not this *too* much to believe? Is it possible that every crushing experience of life can be attributed to the sovereign Lord of all? Even more than that, can such sorrows and disasters become stepping-stones to greater heights of spiritual experience?

For many a storm-tossed believer this problem has assumed such magnitude that we may profitably consider the facts in the light of Scripture, for until the problem is resolved we shall fail to enjoy the

fullness of the "peace...which passeth all understanding." The Christian who wonders if Satan can
divert him from the path of God's will knows no rest
of mind. He thinks that the harsh and unkind actions
of men may nullify his earnest efforts to glorify God.
He feels that he must fight strenuously to maintain
his reputation when it is being smeared or tarnished
by the unjust criticisms of his brethren. He is distressed and confused when he is unable to enter
through some apparently wide-opened door because
of opposition from others, or through ill health or lack
of finances. How can he see the "hand of God" in
all this? He asks himself, "Is it possible to reconcile
the apparent contradiction of unfavorable circumstances with the doctrine that no 'second causes' can
hinder the progress of the child of God in his onward
path?" Can he subscribe to the words of the following couplet?

> In the center of the circle of the will of God I
>     stand;
> I can own no second causes, all must come from
>     His dear hand.

The Book of Job undoubtedly gives an affirmative
answer. Job's trials show us plainly that where there
is true submission to the will of God, no second
causes can hinder the working of God's grace in the
spiritual growth and sanctification of the believer.
As in *Pilgrim's Progress*, Satan may pour water
defiantly on the fire of the Christian's faith, but behind it all, Christ is seen to be pouring on more than
adequate supplies of oil, so that the fire burns more
brightly than ever. All the forces that Satan can

mobilize against the child of God can affect only the apparent and outward trend of his life, while behind the scenes God waits like a refiner of silver to use the outwitted Enemy as a means of producing the gracious fruit of the Spirit in a crushed and humbled life.

But does the rest of Scripture confirm this, or is it merely inferred in the Book of Job? What of Paul's confident affirmation, "We know that *all* things work together for good to them that love God, to them who are the called according to his purpose..." (Rom. 8:28)? Not that all things work together into a rose-colored pattern that we should have chosen for ourselves, but rather that all things, whether sweet or bitter, encouraging or frustrating, when accepted as God's plan for the development of our faith, even though they come in the guise of a "messenger of Satan to buffet" us, can result only in a more fragrant life as we learn with Paul in his trials that God's grace is sufficient for us.

Again remember the aged Jacob, a distressed and defeated patriarch in the throes of a bitter trial, as he cries, "Joseph is not, Simeon is not." And now Benjamin's life is threatened by mysterious circumstances over which Jacob has no control and through which he sees no daylight. The future appears so menacing and hopeless that he moans, "All these things are against me." How little he knew! Little did he realize that this new threat to his security would result in the great thrill of seeing his best-loved and long-lost son again, not only alive but elevated to a position of rank and wealth from which he could supply every need of the distressed patriarch. And had the "second causes" in the life of Joseph frustrated the purposes of God? Certainly God did not put into the hearts of his brothers that bitter hatred which was the immediate reason for his unenviable experiences in the pit and the prison, but God did *permit* it, and then displayed His unquestioned mastery of the situation by granting to Joseph the all-sufficient grace which upheld him through the darkest hours of his trials and which produced in him that singular sweetness of character and purity of life which brought him into such conspicuous favor with God and man. As Jacob embraced his beloved Joseph and slowly took in the scene of pomp and grandeur which surrounded his son as the prime minister of Egypt, and heard the grateful thanks of the whole nation expressed as they were sustained during the long famine by the corn in the royal storehouses, how trivial and petty would seem his peevish cry, "All these things are against me"!

Oh, may God grant to us the grace to claim this lofty mountaintop of faith as our rightful stance, from which we shall be "above" and not "under" the varied circumstances of life. Even as Job (who had not the solace and confirmation of the written Word of God), may we realize that when we cannot reconcile the apparent paradoxes of life with what we expected to receive, the secret of peace and contentment is to proclaim boldly, "The hand of God hath wrought this!"

7. *His longing for God* (23:3). "Oh that I knew where I might find HIM!" With intense longing his soul cried out for God. David, too, experienced that holy, fervent craving in the wilderness of Judah as he cried out, "O God, thou art my God; early will I seek *thee*: my soul thirsteth for *thee*, my flesh longeth for *thee* . . . . to see *thy* power and *thy* glory, . . . *thy*

lovingkindness is better than life, my lips shall praise
*thee....*I remember *thee...*and meditate on
*thee...."* (Psalm 63).

Paul also in familiar words declares the same
intensity of passion as the highest ambition of his
eager soul, "That I may know *him...*" (Phil. 3:10).
For these noble souls there is no longer a fleshly
craving for the blessings of the Christian life, no mere
lust for the many "by-products" of the Gospel, but
an all-consuming passion to "know HIM."

> My goal is *God Himself*, not joy, nor peace,
>   Not even blessing, but Himself, my God;
> 'Tis His to lead me there—not mine, but His—
>   At any cost, dear Lord, by any road.
>
> So faith bounds forward to its goal in God,
>   And love can trust her Lord to lead her there;
> Upheld by Him, my soul is following hard
>   Till God hath full fulfilled my deepest prayer.
>
> No matter if the way be sometimes dark,
>   No matter though the cost be oft-times great,
> He knoweth how I best shall reach the mark,
>   The way that leads to Him must needs be
>     straight.
>
> One thing I know, I cannot say Him nay;
>   One thing I do, I press towards my Lord;
> My God my glory here, from day to day,
>   And in the glory there my great Reward.

To his critics, who maintain that Job is a hypocrite,
Job throws out a strong challenge: "Will he [the
hypocrite] *delight* himself in the Almighty?" (27:8-
10). The suffering patriarch assures his friends

ardently that real satisfaction is not found in mere "things," however precious they may be, for now in the depths of sorrow and deprivation he can say with all the passion of his soul, "I delight in HIM."

May it be ours to know Him, so that not glibly but with the earnest devotion of a Job, a David, or a Paul, we may sing:

> Thou my everlasting Portion,
> More than friend or life to me,
> All along my pilgrim journey,
> Saviour, let me walk with Thee.

8. *He looks to God alone for justice* (31:35). Since God alone matters to a man stripped of every earthly prop, Job says, "My desire is, that the Almighty would answer me, . . ." "My friends fail me, Satan buffets me, so I look to God for justice; I appeal to 'the Judge of all the earth'!"

9. *His understanding of the power of God in creation* (chapter 26).

Job invites Bildad to descend with him to Sheol and view the dead confined there (vv. 5-6); then, in imagination standing apart, to look at the earth suspended in space (v. 7); then, to survey the immense ocean of water enveloping the earth in cloud-form (vv. 8-9); then, the ocean disposed around the earth, and therefore appearing alternately in light and darkness as the earth revolves (v. 10); then, to consider the mighty laws that maintain the celestial bodies in their orbits (v. 11); then, the Divine power that restrains the oceans in their respective beds, controlling their proud waves (v. 12); and, lastly, he invites Bildad to understand, if he can, the wisdom that beautifies the heavens with stars, and particularly the great constellation Serpens.

In verse 14, Job declares that these are only parts, or outlines of His ways, "a little portion," that is, a mere whisper of them, and he asks, "Who then can comprehend the thunder of His power, if unable to understand His mere whisperings?" (*Student's Commentary on the Holy Scriptures.*)

10. *His immediate response to God* (40:3-6; 42:1-6). In his anguish, Job has said many heated things which in his better moments would never have passed his lips, but this was not characteristic of Job. When finally and conclusively God broke His silence and brought the battle of words to a suitable climax, the response of Job was spontaneous and complete submission to God.

We have thus noted some of the dominant points which stand out like lighthouses in the gloom, indicating the true quality of Job's faith, his wide knowledge of spiritual truths, and his loyalty and whole-hearted devotion to God.

Nothing could shake his love for God, and he was thus able to demonstrate the truth of words written thousands of years later, "Love...endureth all things...never faileth."

CHAPTER FOUR

# The Revelation of the "Flesh" in a Godly Man

JOB WAS A TRUE MAN OF GOD. Of this we have adequate proof, not only in the outward life which his fellowmen observed but also in the secrets of his inner life, known only to God, who pronounced those wonderful words of commendation, "There is none like him in the earth." Moreover, it was not a fleeting, spasmodic experience in his life to walk with God, for at the time we meet him in this fascinating story he was already a man with long experience in the life of faith. Yes, Job was godly. He was great. He was a mature saint, one who, like Enoch, walked with God and had this testimony that he pleased God!

And yet Job had much to learn of hitherto unsuspected depths of evil in his own sinful heart. As we pay earnest and sympathetic attention to the spectacle of the great and godly Job in his trials, pounded with a pestle in the mortar of suffering, we notice that although there were some stirring exhibitions of his true faith and spiritual maturity, there were also many reactions that were *not* commendable—ugly things that indicate the hideous nature of the self-life, even in such a saint.

With sincerity and humility, let us endeavor to tabulate some of the more obvious traits of the "flesh" as they appear in Job's utterances, so that we may learn to appreciate the awfulness of these things which are so natural to us. We dare not study Job's self-life in a pharisaical spirit, but as men in like mold we may ask the Holy Spirit of Truth to use this study to make bare the evil of our own sinful hearts, for every honest student must confess that many of the unenviable things in Job's experience also appear in us and often with much less justification.

1. *Discontent and impatience.* For seven silent days and weary nights, Job sits on the ash heap, almost numbed by the suddenness and severity of his trials. Gradually the full weight of his afflictions comes home to him in an overwhelming flood of sorrow and suffering until, upon our astonished ears, the voice of Job falls in accents strange and harsh. "He opened his mouth and bitterly cursed his [birth-] day." Why was I ever born? Why did I ever see the light of day? Why did I ever grow to manhood?

"Why, Job," we ask in surprise, "have you forgotten those many years of happiness, prosperity, and spiritual blessing? Have you forgotten a whole lifetime enriched by God's bountiful favor which made your life the envy of your fellowmen and which incurred the malice of the satanic hosts?" But wait! We have no need to ask Job to answer that for us, because as we think for a moment we remember only too well that we are ever ready to do just the same thing. The years of sweet fellowship with God and His saints, the abundant answers to prayer, the joy in His service, all add up to an impressive total that we could never forget. But let one severe blow fall upon us, and the light goes out! We grow discontented and impatient, quick to forget the goodness and mercy that have followed us all the days of our lives. How quickly has Job forgotten God's protecting grace—the "hedge" which had made him invulnerable for a lifetime, the very thing which was the occasion for the present hate of Satan against him! When tears bedim our vision, we forget, too, that "weeping may endure for a night, but joy cometh in the morning." So, penitently we stand beside Job, convicted of our own frequent participation in the prevalent but peace-destroying habit of impatient grumblings at our lot in life.

2. *Inconsistency.* Doubtless Job did not realize the inconsistency in his life until it was driven home to his bewildered heart by the unexpectedly harsh retort of his dear old friend, Eliphaz. "Job, you are the one who has comforted many in grief, you have strengthened the weak hands with words that rang true to God, you have encouraged many in their affliction—*but now,* it has happened to you, and you burst out into wild words cursing your misfortune! Is this your fear, your confidence, your hope?" (4:3-6). Cruel words, and ill-timed indeed, yet there was a germ of truth in them. We are always ready to offer advice and comfort to others, quick to urge them to look to God for help and consolation, but it is not easy to practice what we preach; it is natural to show inconsistency at the first sign of trial.

3. *Job withdraws from his earlier surrender to the will of God* (6:8-9). Job now takes the line of least resistance, saying as it were, "I am not willing to endure this; it is far easier to die than to go on in this agony." That he is not alone in this retreat from

the will of God is common knowledge to every honest
believer and has been summed up by the poet in the
familiar words:

> Teach me to live, 'tis easier far to die—
>   Gently and silently to pass away—
> On earth's long night to close the heavy eye,
>   And waken in the glorious realms of day.

In the fervent warmth of surrender to God we are
quite ready to sing, "Where He leads me I will follow,
I'll go with Him, with Him, all the way," but when
God accepts our surrender and begins to lead us into
the heat of the refining fires or into the valley of
humiliation, the "flesh" is quick to reassert itself;
we regret our bold profession of loyalty to Christ
and make a cowardly retreat from the high stand
of surrender to the will of God. But we learn through
bitter experience that there is no joy in this.

4. *Self-pity* (7:11). "I will complain. . ." Prob-
ably no manifestation of the self-life is more corrosive
and damaging to the soul than indulgence in self-
pity, and yet in all its myriad forms it *seems* so harm-
less. Job did not find any relief from his sorrows,
nor did he add to his happiness by complaining of his
woes. The child of God is never secure from this
temptation. He says to himself, "I have tried *so*
hard; I did my best, but everything has gone wrong"
and, sitting down to nurse his injured feelings, he
echoes Job's words, "I will complain." He had felt
so confident of his own spirituality and ability that
he smugly *expected* to be chosen for some position
of honor or prominence. But he was overlooked;
some other was preferred before him, and at once

the "flesh," ever eager for an opportunity to gain the ascendency over the "new man," bestirs itself and says, "If I am not appreciated, I give up; I quit; I will complain! If I cannot be the chairman, or the secretary, or the preacher, or the song leader or the soloist, then I have every right to complain, and complain I will!" Perhaps it takes the form of discontent with our lot in life; others seem to prosper and succeed, but for us nothing goes as we would wish.

We must admit that Job had more justification for his complaint than we do, but even the desire to tabulate the varying degrees of "justification" is so obviously a trait of the "flesh" that we would do well to ask God to show us if self-pity is keeping us from glorifying Him. Not for Paul the complaining attitude! "I have learned," he says, "in whatsoever state I am, therewith to be content" (Phil. 4:11). May He grant to us the grace to resist the destructive force of self-centered vainglory and to be willing to esteem others better than ourselves, "that in all things he might have the preeminence."

5. *Confused thinking* (10:15). How frail indeed is the mortal frame! The most noble spirit dwells in a home of clay, and when that fragile house is stricken with disease, weakness, or pain, the spirit can be so easily enshrouded in mists that cloud the vision. The spirit struggles to rise on wings of faith, to abide in the will of God, but the suffering body cannot follow, and the whole man sinks into a state of confusion. He knows not what to think, knows not how to pray! "Did God send this heavy stroke? Is it a punishment for my sin? Am I out of the will of God? I am willing to confess my sin, but what is it? No specific transgression presses on my conscience, yet

the heavens are as brass; the Bible does not bring me a glimmer of light for my disordered ways. What is the matter?" Surely these were Job's inner thoughts as he groaned, "I am full of confusion!" Yet Job lived to teach us that such confusion is only the failure of the man to grasp the thoughts of God that are higher than the heavens above.

6. *Fearful anxiety* (9:27-35). Job is now in a very unhappy state. Conscious of, and condemned by, his own fleshly mutterings, he seems to lose his assurance of salvation, the sheet anchor of the saint and, like many another pilgrim, he falls into the grip of Giant Despair of Doubting Castle. He says, "I am afraid of life with its sufferings; I am afraid of death and judgment." Perhaps every believer does not have fears as clearly defined as these, yet most of us know the bitter experience of doubt, when our joy is lost, our vision clouded, and our horizons befogged with foul vapors of fear, which certainly are of the "flesh" because "perfect love casteth out fear" (I John 4:18).

Much ink has been used on definitions and explanations of the occurrence of fear, anxiety, and worry in the life of a believer and the antidote for these hateful things. Fear and worry are as natural to some as jubilant optimism is to others, but as ever, that which is natural must be subordinated to that which is spiritual if the child of God is to enjoy abundant life. The jubilant optimist must learn that his natural effervescence can be just as destructive to a walk in dependence upon God's will as the fears and worries of the child of God who may, like Fearing in *Pilgrim's Progress,* go through the Valley of Humiliation more easily than his robust brother. Some of the greatest of saints, whose devotion to Christ is beyond

question, cannot rise above anxiety and worry over
their loved ones and other allied subjects. "Don't
worry," says one. "Trust in God; He looks after
them." The worried soul replies, "I *do* trust God,
but nowhere does He promise me that I shall not
be afflicted with all the woes common to man." The
Christian's faith is no guarantee against illness, ac-
cident, bereavements and the heartrending disappoint-
ments of life. Surely the answer to fearful anxiety is
not a glib "Trust in God." Rather it lies in complete
acceptance of God's will and a faith which rises to
believe that any losses we may sustain can lead us
only into deeper fellowship with God. This faith says,
"God does not promise us immunity from sorrow,
but He *does* promise grace to endure the trial laid
upon us in His unfathomable but ever-loving purpose." For Job and for every saint the only sure
foundation for deliverance from this snare is the Word
of God.

7. *Utter discouragement* (10:18). Job reckons
his life to be useless. To what purpose is life under
such conditions? Discouragement is deadly. The story
—or more correctly, the parable—has been told
that when Satan was holding a clearance sale of all his
weapons and instruments, he retained one wedge-
shaped instrument called "discouragement," which
he considered the most effective in his possession. Of
course, Job is not alone in his discouragement. See the
great and rugged Elijah! He sat down under the juni-
per tree "and requested for himself that he might die,"
saying, "It is enough; now, O LORD, take away my
life" (I Kings 19:4). Or think of Jonah, who "wished
in himself to die, and said, It is better for me to die
than to live" (Jonah 4:8). Think of other great men—

no, let us simply look into our own hearts and remember the times without number when, utterly discouraged, we have been ready to give in, to lay down our weapons and begin a cowardly retreat from the purposes of God for us. From our privileged position as those who have the guidance of the Word of God, let us shout the message out loud and clear, "Jonah, Elijah, Job! This is only a passing circumstance! Job, you shall yet know greater honor and blessing than ever before. Elijah, your work is not over, God has planned great tasks for you; you have yet to anoint kings and prophets. Jonah, before you lies a mighty ministry as a man who has seen God at work." The bitter experience is only transient, but the "flesh" is too shortsighted to see what James calls "the end of the Lord" (James 5:11).

The Malays have a proverb in which a man is likened to a frog sitting underneath a coconut husk, convinced that the husk is the sky. He thinks that the world is a small place because he can see nothing beyond his husk. It is a very telling illustration of shortsightedness. In our trial we look only at the immediate environment and, like the frog, we arrive at the conclusion that all is dark. Certainly it is dark under the husk, but outside the sun still shines on a vast world of beauty, and had we but the faith to venture forth from the confined limits of our "husk," we would realize that the shadow of the passing circumstance only lends color to the constant light of God's grace and blessing.

Ye trembling saints, fresh courage take!
The clouds ye so much dread

Are big with mercy; and shall break
In blessings on your head.

8. *Job accuses God of injustice.* "He multiplieth my wounds without a cause" (9:17). "Wherefore hidest thou thy face?" (13:24). While still holding to his earlier belief that it was the hand of God that smote him, he now complains that the smiting is unjust, without a cause, and that God hides from him; that even though he cries out to God, He will neither listen to nor regard his prayers (30:20).

9. *"Odious" comparisons* (13:2). In such a state of despair, when the soul cannot understand the ways of God, the "flesh" readily seeks to excuse its ways and bolster up its case by making comparisons. Fellow believers come with a desire to console and encourage us by turning us to the Word of God, which should be an exercise very much to our profit. But what happens? The "flesh," ever ready to resent any implied or—more frequently—imagined superiority, bestirs itself and retorts proudly, "I know all that; I am not inferior to you," and thus something which might have become a stepping-stone to victory becomes to the self-life just one more burden to be carried.

10. *He asks God to leave him alone* (14:1-6). "Turn from me—leave me alone in peace." Poor Job! What a thoroughly fleshly desire! We see it even in the unregenerate, as Job himself points out when in chapter 21, verse 14, he depicts men as saying, "Depart from us; for we desire not the knowledge of thy ways." That is natural! The unconverted man wants to be left alone in his own sinful way, a fact confirmed by Eliphaz in chapter 22, verse 17: "Depart

from us:...what can the Almighty do for them?"
In our ignorance, we do not *want* God nor do we
consider that we *need* Him. But God is the Creator,
a God whose very nature is love, and He cannot and
will not leave His own creatures to perish blindly.
Therefore God sent forth His Son to seek and to
save that which was lost. When confronted with that
fact, in the person of Jesus Christ, and overcome
by a sense of His majesty, Peter, a fitting representa-
tive of our race, bursts out with the same natural cry,
"Depart from me; for I am a sinful man, O Lord,"
to which Jesus replied (if we may reverently para-
phrase His words), "No, Peter, I will not depart
from you. If I did, you would be unfit for My
presence forever. You follow Me and depart from
your sin." Peter saw the logic of it and felt the at-
traction of the purity of God's Son and he arose, left
all, and came to Christ, compared with whom all the
world is loss.

Even today men, unchanged in heart since the time
of Job, are saying defiantly, "Depart from us!" while
with infinite patience the Lord ever answers, "Come
unto Me." Impelled by that constraining love, we
come. In coming we find rest unto our souls, and in
the joy of that experience we sing,

> Have Thine own way Lord! Have Thine own way!
> Hold o'er my being absolute sway!

The Lord cannot be satisfied with anything less than
holiness in the lives of His children and so, taking us
at our word, He begins to have His way in dealing
with the corrupt "flesh." But the old nature has no
desire to die, and we immediately find a carnal reac-

tion rising in our hearts. We cry out, "I didn't expect
*this;* the Christian life is *too* hard, the refining process
is *too* humbling. I expected joy and peace and thrilling service, but this is too much! O Lord, leave me
alone, just let me be an *ordinary* Christian!" Sometimes it would appear that He accedes to our peevish
petition for mediocrity, and sends leanness into our
souls.

Yet could we be satisfied with such an experience?
Let us rather seek grace to continue to pray, "Have
Thine own way," and give Him the right to continue
His painful but gracious work of purging and pruning
that there may be fruit, more fruit—yes, much fruit
in lives that rejoice in the sense of His constant
presence.

11. *A rhapsody in defense of self.* Beginning from
chapter 29, verse 1, Job commences a summing-up
of his own case as seen through his own eyes. He
is plainly occupied with himself right through the three
chapters until, with a burst of enthusiasm, he declares
emphatically, "The words of Job are ended!" Let us
take note of these three chapters which reveal the
prominent place taken by self, even in the life of a
godly man.

a. *The "I" of prosperity* (29). More than fifty
times the personal pronouns "I," "me," and "my"
occur in this chapter as Job recalls his past blessings. God was not excluded—no, indeed, for there
are frequent references to God's favor and blessing. But beyond all question, it was the "I" who
filled the center of the picture which Job sketched
for his friends. To take but one example, notice
verse 18: "Then *I* said, *I* shall die in *my* nest and
*I* shall multiply *my* days...."

b. *The "I" of adversity* (30). As he summarizes the experiences and disasters which had humbled him so suddenly, there is an increasing emphasis on self, for no less than sixty times the "I" appears in this chapter, showing how self-pity, as we have noticed, causes the capital pronoun to loom very large in the thoughts.

c. *The "I" of innocency* (31). Having emphasized his past prosperity, and restated his present adversity, Job almost "boils over" as he protests his innocency. In this parade of his virtues, he breaks all records by referring to the great "I" about seventy times. There is an ever present danger when we dare to begin a recital of our own virtues, and we are well advised to give heed to Solomon's warning, "Let another man praise thee and not thine own mouth."

Thus self is the keynote of his final reply to his three friends.

The "I" of prosperity ⎫
The "I" of adversity ⎬ were all equally the flesh.
The "I" of innocency ⎭

"Job had yet to learn that self must die, whether it be prosperous self, or afflicted self, or innocent self; and, that he had to be brought to abhor himself, whether innocent or guilty. Entrance into the life more abundant can only be experienced when religious self is as heartily abhorred as the irreligious self." (*Student's Commentary.*)

It was not until Job, the upright, began to justify himself to his friends that he opened the doors to his inmost being and brought to light the truly monstrous "I" which dwelt within. In these three chapters we recognize many of the fleshly mutterings of the carnal man in our own experience. Conspicuous among them is the self-confidence already noted (29:18-20). He felt that he had achieved security, honor, and satisfaction—in fact, every blessing, and was talking to himself in almost the same language as the rich fool in Luke 12. To the "natural man" this attitude is quite justifiable, even commendable, and it is a slow and painful task learning the lesson that the believer is to live no longer on the natural plane.

12. *A longing for "the good old days."* This is just one more subtle manifestation of the activity of the self-life. "Why, what is wrong with that?" queries a perplexed soul. Notice then! Job says, "Oh, for those good old days when God preserved me" (29:2). "Oh, for those happy days of my youth" (29:4-7). Oh, they were wonderful, blessed days of Heaven on earth! "BUT NOW" (30:1) "AND NOW" (30:9-10). Ah, yes! "But now," sighed Job as he compared the glorious past with the tragic present. Surely it was a perfectly natural thing to do! Yes, but let us pause for a moment's reflection. What has God recorded for us, for our instruction, concerning those palmy days of prosperity and blessing and happiness? Nothing, not a word, but a whole book to describe those brief days of trial! Had Job only known that for thousands of years countless numbers of distressed believers would derive comfort and enlightenment from the record of his trials and losses, he would not have groaned so bitterly about the unfavorable comparison between the "good old days" and "now."

Surely, then, morbid longings for the past and its blessings have no right to appear in the life of the believer. With great gusto we sing, "Every day with

Jesus is sweeter than the day before." If we realize that for some reason we are beginning to think that the past experiences of joy and blessedness are more real than our present state, it is time for an immediate and thorough appraisal of our spiritual condition. The glorious hope of the child of God is in the *future* —not in the *past,* while the *present* is just a stepping-stone on the way heavenward. The final blessedness of the Christian is not to be found in the degree of success or prosperity he enjoys, even though allied with godliness, but rather in the fact that "we have fellowship with Him." It is the presence of our risen Lord which transforms every trial into a triumph! Think again of those familiar but ever fresh words of David who sang, "The Lord is my shepherd; ...though I walk through the valley... *Thou art with me.*" Does it not shed a ray of glory upon the darkest path in the deepest valley to remember that our God has revealed Himself as *Jehovah Shammah* (The Lord is there)? Yes, just *there* where we need Him most! Once again, we quote familiar words, "Where He leads me I will follow,...I'll go *with Him, with Him* all the way." Nothing else and nothing less than the assurance that the Lord is there could inspire a weak mortal to dare to leave all and tread an unknown way—just wherever He may lead.

"Lo, I am with you alway, even unto the end..." In this confidence we ought not to waste time in bemoaning the "good old days." Rather we ought to give earnest heed to the testimony of Paul in his bold and spirited declaration, "Forgetting those things which are behind,...I press toward the mark for the prize of the high calling of God in Christ Jesus." Not for Paul the valiant those pathetic bleatings about the

past days of ease and fame! His eyes were fixed on
the goal ahead. "This is my desire, that I may know
Him, that I might be like Him, that I might be with
Him. All else is but refuse!"

> So even I, and with a heart more burning,
>    So even I, and with a hope more sweet,
> Groan for the hour, O Christ! of Thy returning,
>    Faint for the flaming of Thine advent feet.

> Yea thro' life, death, thro' sorrow and thro' sinning
>    He shall suffice me, for He hath sufficed:
> Christ is the end, for Christ was the beginning,
>    Christ the beginning, for the end is Christ.
>                    "St. Paul," by F. W. H. Myers

In concluding this consideration of the natural and
fleshly weaknesses of Job, we observe two main les-
sons emerging from the study. First, we have gained a
new realization of the fact that in the pathway of
discipline and trial we learn by bitter experience the
truth of Paul's confession, "In me...in my flesh
dwelleth no good thing." Coupled with that is the
lesson that God waits with infinite patience, like the
potter, to work out a design of grace and beauty with
such frail material.

# CHAPTER FIVE

# *Elihu Answers*

THE WORDS OF JOB are ended." In one of his earlier
discourses Job had desired that his own words might
be recorded forever, written in a book or carved in
solid rock (19:23-24). But in his last impassioned
outburst, he cried out, "Oh,...that *mine adversary*
had written a book!" (31:35). His final challenge
was, in effect, "Show me why I should suffer like this;
write it down so that I can study it. Could I but have
the divine reply, I would bind it as a crown to me"
(31:36). But God does not answer, and silence falls
upon the little group. Job has nothing further to say.
His three friends have roundly berated Job and condemned him as a hypocrite, although they proved incapable of answering his questions.

All this time, Elihu sat there listening silently, but
when the great controversialists lapse into silence also,
he can endure it no longer. His earnestness overcomes
the natural Eastern reticence of youth in the presence
of age and, like a bursting wineskin, his words pour
out in a torrent of eloquence which commands the
attention of his elders. "Job," he cries, "listen to me!
You have demanded that God should answer you!
Why, I am but a clay vessel like you, but I can see

many discrepancies in your arguments. There is an answer to your problem; allow me to speak!"

In spite of his modest protestations of youthful inexperience, Elihu was obviously a man of spiritual maturity. From his spirited address we learn:

1. *He is indignant at the attitude displayed by Job* (32:2; 34:36-37).

2. *He is indignant with the three friends* (32:3).

3. *He offers himself as a mediator* (33:6). He was generous enough to realize that Job was not at his best; his state was such that he had become incapable of clear reasoning; a mediator was a necessity to renew his mental appreciation of the true ways of God.

4. *He asks why Job should dare to demand an explanation from God* (33:13). Must God give an account of His matters? Is God accountable to Job or has Job the right to demand an audit? Is it not possible that God should have a wise purpose in matters that seem unjust to finite man? "He that is perfect in knowledge" is surely above the querulous demands of His creatures.

5. *He shows that God is concerned with man's spiritual profit* (33:29-30). Since God's dealings are directed toward the highest and the ultimate good of His creatures, we may not know the wisdom that guides our way until we reach the Father's home, until that day "when the crooked ways are straightened, and the dark things shall be plain."

6. *He indicates where Job has failed* (34:9). Even to mortal eyes it was clear that Job had misconstrued the facts. Without realizing it, Job had argued himself into a false position where he was perilously near

to using the words of Satan when he first laid a charge against him. Satan had said, "Doth Job fear God for nought?" And now Job himself had conveyed the impression that service to God should merit favor, that gain should follow godliness! "It profiteth me nothing. . . ."

7. *He shows that God could not be unjust* (34:12, 17, 19, 23). Because He is holy, He cannot be unjust; moreover, He is merciful and will not lay upon man more than he can bear (I Cor. 10:13).

8. *He shows that God teaches through chastisement* (34:31-32; 36:10). "Now no chastening for the present seemeth to be joyous, but grievous: nevertheless afterward it yieldeth the peaceable fruit of righteousness to them that are exercised thereby" (Heb. 12:11). Elihu wisely points out that by seeking to know the will of God concerning the *purpose* of the chastisement we may the more speedily learn the lesson our Father desires to teach us and thus shorten the period of the testing, for once the lesson is learned, there is no further need for the chastisement to continue. It is natural to ask, "*When* shall I get out of this trial?" But, to enter into the fullest blessing, we should rather ask, "*What* shall I get out of it?" Then, with Job, we shall find our trials to be channels of grace and blessing. The moment Job learned his lesson and realized the utter worthlessness of self, the trial was over!

9. *He shows that Job has lost his song* (35:10-11). Job had not shown greater intelligence than the animal creation; he failed to raise a "song in the night." Paul and Silas succeeded in this test!

Elihu's whole argument may be summarized as follows: Job is incapable of understanding the ways of

God in nature; how much less can he comprehend the all-wise purposes of God in dealing with His creatures? Whether Elihu intended to say more, we do not know, for at this stage in the discussion God spoke.

# CHAPTER SIX

# *The Answer of Jehovah to Job*

*"Then the* LORD *answered Job out of the whirlwind..."* (38:1). How strange, and yet how wonderful that after all that had happened, God should choose to speak from the *whirlwind.* Where did we last see the wind play a part in the narrative? It was the wind that had been the means of destroying Job's most precious treasures, his children. Now, when God breaks the long silence to end the debate and fully vindicate His beloved servant, He speaks out of the whirlwind. Did Job at once discern the great truth which to us is so plain? It was the wind that slew his sons and daughters, but herein is mystery, *God was in the wind!*

Our minds go to another distressing incident in the New Testament. The disciples were out on the lake, alone and in distress. Around them the storm howled and raged. The water rose in foaming billows which terrified them, hindered their progress, and threatened to engulf them. Yet in that moment of darkness and dread, their beloved Master came to them, *walking on the water.* They would never have thought that on that boisterous water which was the reason for their terror their Lord and Master would approach them, but so it was. The water was under His feet—yes, under His control! So it was most surely with the whirlwind, and Job was right when he uttered those fine words, "The hand of God hath touched me" (19:21).

The prophet Nahum remarks, "The LORD hath his way in the whirlwind" (Nahum 1:3). God often reveals Himself where we least expect to find Him. When Elijah was hiding in his cave and had to be brought to a realization of his failure and his need, there passed by a great and mighty wind, but "the Lord was not in the wind" (I Kings 19:11). But years later, when the earthly ministry of Elijah was ended and God translated him from earth to glory, the divine agent was the wind! Elijah went up to Heaven in a whirlwind.

From this brief digression concerning God's ways with men, we are to learn, surely, that no man should presume to dogmatize on God's ways and methods. He is the true Despot, who giveth not account of His matters. Whether He speaks out of the whirlwind or with that "still small voice," the method matters little provided we realize that He, in His sovereign wisdom, will use the particular means best suited to shed light on our pathway and, at the same time, to teach us that He is "not far from any one of us." May we be like Samuel of the attentive ear, ready to say, "Speak; for thy servant heareth."

As the voice of God broke the stillness, what thoughts must have surged through the hearts of all the participants in that long and wordy argument!

God spoke directly to Job and silenced him utterly.

The answer of God was threefold:

1. Can Job explain the works of God?

2. Can Job understand the power of God in creation?

3. Until Job can do this, then let him refrain from questioning God's wisdom or justice in His moral government of the creatures which are the work of His hands (40:2).

## The Answer of Job to Jehovah

Face to face at last with God, in whom his faith had been rooted even though he only dimly discerned parts of His ways, Job at once admits his failure and folly. His spoken reply, in striking contrast to his long-winded protestations of innocence and virtue before his friends, is brief and to the point!

1. *I am vile* (40:4). He does not need to be told of his own corruption; it is all too obvious as he lies in the presence of unsullied holiness. Like Isaiah (Isaiah 6), the only expression that rises to his lips is that unfeigned "I am vile."

2. *God's ways are too wonderful* (42:3). With the new unveiling of the ways of God, Job is amazed at his own temerity in ever daring to raise a peevish cry against the One whose ways are perfect.

3. *I see Thee,* i.e., I understand (42:5). "In Thy presence I cease from my intellectual gropings; I am convinced; I see Thee in everything. I see not yet Thy purpose but I see Thee!"

4. *"Wherefore I abhor myself."* Like Moses, like Isaiah, like Daniel, or John on the isle of Patmos, Job finds that the vision of God causes all else to fade from sight. His friends and their calumnies, his own fervent attempts at self-justification, his loud pleas for justice—all are forgotten as Job falls to

the ground. As he lies there in the direct blaze of the holiness of God, the soul of Job rises to a new height of spiritual perception and he cries out, "I abhor myself and repent in dust and ashes." Of what did he repent? No mention is made of any specific sin; no evil deeds are suggested over which he need distress his soul in deep contrition. No, Job was a just man, a justified man, but seeing himself now in the light of God's holiness, he repents of all the carnal thoughts which had passed through his mind while he had been occupied with self. Lying there before God, just where he had longed to be (23:3), he learns the unfathomable depths of corruption in all that he had admired in himself. He learns exactly what Paul meant when he exclaimed, "...In my flesh dwelleth no good thing," and that which was in the mind of Solomon when he spoke of "the plague of his own heart."

Let us ponder a moment. Who is this lying there in such humility and grief, grief not now over his sorrows but over his utter worthlessness? It is none other than Job, the saintliest man of his day, of whom God had declared, "There is none like him in the earth." We recall the glowing words of divine praise in the opening pages of the story, we remember his former greatness and honor, but, as we observe the new spirit of self-abasement and abhorrence, we are brought to realize (to borrow a famous phrase) that *this* was his "finest hour."

It is significant that the first and last words of Job describe the actual value of human nature and human achievement. The very first words that fell from his lips were, "Naked came I out..." (1:21), and the last we hear him say are "dust and ashes"

(42:6). Having learned *that* truth, there was no need for further refining trials, no need for chastisement to continue. Satan had no other accusation, and dared not make any other insinuation, and is seen no more in the narrative. Whether he was banished by God's express command, or whether he merely slunk away to hide his defeat, matters little now. He could not destroy Job's faith nor shake his loyalty to God, and the very trials by which Satan had hoped to display Job's hypocrisy were the means by which Job was completely vindicated and raised to even higher spiritual and material prosperity.

*     *     *

### The Result

With wonder we realize afresh the great eternal love and grace of God in that He took up Job's case as soon as he came to the end of himself and the end of his gropings, his mutterings, his self-confidence, and his protestations of innocence. It came as a rude awakening to his three friends; it shattered their self-confidence and revealed their ignorance of the true ways of God. Their whole system of theology fell in ruins about them, leaving them openly revealed as the early ancestors of the Pharisees, smugly self-righteous, coldly critical, and carnally confident in their own vaunted knowledge and experience. Even while they were rebuking Job for his supposed sin, they were more culpable than he, for God said, "Ye have not spoken of me the thing that is right, as my servant Job hath" (42:7). "Why not?" we may ask, in an earnest desire to learn from their mistakes. They had discoursed very ably on sin (25:4-6), but *always as it concerned others!* The cutting edge of

their knowledge was never turned inwards! Herein
lies a solemn message for all who read the Scriptures,
and especially for those who teach them. May we be
given grace to apply the Word of God to our own
hearts and lives before we seek to rectify the crooked-
ness that we see in our brethren. "First cast out the
beam out of thine own eye; and then thou shalt see
clearly to cast out the mote out of thy brother's eye"
(Matt. 7:5).

God's condemnation of the words and ways of the
three friends emphasizes the importance of care in
the matter of outspoken criticisms of our brethren,
especially of those who seem to us to be enduring
the heat of the refining fire. Untold harm is done to
the cause of Christ by the horrid, devilish sin of
malicious or even thoughtless criticism of those
around us. We are ever ready to criticize their be-
havior or their activities or lack of activities; we
discourse sanctimoniously on their shallow understanding of spiritual truths; we speak contemptuously
of their disobedience to doctrines which are so plain,
so elementary (to us), without paying any attention to
the fact that our criticisms are based on surmise rather
than facts, for we have no means of knowing the
motives, which appear only to God. Our sense of
importance and our prestige are enhanced artificially
by comparing ourselves with our brethren, especially
when we jump to the conclusion that they are under
God's disciplinary chastisement. We are human and
fallible, for "to err is human." Thus we do well to
pause and consider the stern warning which fell from
the lips of our Lord, ". . . with what measure ye
mete, it shall be measured to you again." What if God
did indeed judge us with the same harsh censure

which we pronounce upon our brethren? After all, they are not answerable to us; they are not our servants. Every man is to give an account of *himself* to God, who knows the secrets of every heart.

Eliphaz, Bildad, and Zophar were blind leaders of the blind. They knew of the Fall of man and its consequences (it was an accepted tenet of their faith), but they did not display a real knowledge of the divine remedy for sin. "How can a man be justified before God?" asks Bildad (25:4). They were either ignorant of, or had failed to avail themselves of, the revealed remedy for sin, for God said to them, "Take a sacrifice for your sins lest I deal with you according to your folly" (42:7-8). Before they could stand before God, a sacrifice must be offered; there must be atonement! Job needed not to offer a sacrifice at this point; he was a justified man and one thus qualified to engage in the priestly task of intercession for his friends. The three men, formerly so voluble and confident, faded out of the story as penitently they "went and did as the LORD commanded them" and offered the sacrifices which were necessary for their forgiveness and salvation.

When Job uttered his cry of penitence (42:6), it really came from his heart. Only a man who had utterly and unreservedly abandoned every vestige of self-confidence, self-righteousness, and self-pity at the feet of his Lord could really rise to the spirit of Christlike forgiveness which Job displayed as he pleaded for the forgiveness of the men who had treated him with such harshness in the hour of his greatest need. That act of intercession was the final proof of Job's contrition, for it was when he prayed for his friends that the Lord "turned the captivity of Job."

At that moment what rejoicing must have taken place in the presence of the angels as the blessed result of the dread process of sifting became obvious to the hosts in glory! Those angelic beings, in their attendance upon the throne of God, had been present when Satan made his first audacious demand for power to tempt Job. They may have heard the carnal grumblings of Job during the dark period of eclipse and wondered what the final outcome would be. But now there was no doubt at all! The angels would repeat the refrain, "He hath done all things well," for out of the gloom and sorrow caused by the animosity of the Enemy shines the rainbow in the cloud! The grace of God was more than sufficient for Job in all his trials, and from the ash heap rises the patriarch, purer and nobler than ever.

We are not surprised to read of his subsequent prosperity! God could trust Job with greater riches than ever before, for in a man so purified by trials, there was no possibility that his wealth and fame could be used for selfish ends. So "the LORD gave Job twice as much as he had before" (42:10).

By contrast with the overflowing grace of God, what a picture of human nature is given in the first word of verse 11! "THEN"—after his prosperity had been restored. "THEN came there unto him all his brethren, and all his sisters, and all they that had been of his acquaintance before, and did eat bread with him in his house: and they bemoaned him, and comforted him over all the evil that the Lord had brought upon him: every man also gave him a piece of money, and every one an earring of gold." Where

were all these loving relatives when he was sitting on
the ash heap? Where was all their kind commiseration
when he needed it most? Not a word in Scripture
suggested their existence until now.

> Laugh, and the world laughs with you;
> Weep, and you weep alone!

But no reproach falls from the lips of Job. Their
callousness is forgiven and forgotten, and he wel-
comes them magnanimously to the circle of fellowship once more.

Thus we take our leave of Job in his renewed
prosperity, surrounded by family and friends. Job's
life is a permanent monument to the gracious and all-
wise purposes of God.

> Thus this book sets out the action of God in
> leading His children into a higher Christian ex-
> perience. The subject of the book is not how God
> justifies a sinner, but how He sanctifies a saint;
> and hence none but a good man could have been
> chosen for the process, or profited by it. It is
> plain to all that a wicked man should die to self,
> but that a perfect man should also need to die, is
> not so clear. And yet this is the offense of the
> Cross. All that goodness and beauty which men
> recognize in themselves, and in others, must be
> nailed in death to the Cross; and the only Man
> that is to live must be the risen man, Christ Jesus.
> True self-abhorrence comes not from self-exami-
> nation, but in looking away from self to Jesus, the
> Perfecter as well as the Author of faith. Job was
> very much satisfied with himself until he saw God.
> "Self" is very enticing to man, especially religious
> self, and self-examination is an interesting occupa-

tion, and accordingly it is found very difficult to
learn the lesson to crucify it; and to find that
victory is enjoyed only when self is ignored and
Christ adored. (*Students' Commentary on the Holy
Scriptures.*)

EPILOGUE

# The Book of Job and the New Testament

WE HAVE ALREADY NOTED the view expressed by some students that the Book of Job may be the oldest religious book in existence. If this is so, it is indeed striking that such an ancient book should deal with the sanctification of the believer, a doctrine which has proved to be utterly obnoxious to men through the whole history of the human race. The "flesh" rebels against such a doctrine and would gladly dispose of it. To relegate this teaching to past ages would be easy were it not for the fact that the New Testament is fully in line with the Book of Job. As a fitting conclusion to our study, let us note the main outlines of the teaching of the Book of Job as they appear in the New Testament, clearly set out for us who live in this present age of grace.

1. *The person and work of Satan is revealed plainly.* Time and space forbid an adequate treatment of this subject and it will be sufficient to note several important references: In Revelation 12:10 Satan is termed "the accuser of the brethren." In I Peter 5:8 we see "the devil as a roaring lion, [who] walketh about seeking whom he may devour." Ephesians 6:11-12 describes Satan as full of "wiles" and the great enemy against whom the believer must war.

2. *The godly are tested.* We cannot do better than refer to our great Example, the Lord Jesus Christ, who is our pattern in all things. Of Him we read, "Though he were a Son, yet learned he obedience by the things which he suffered" (Heb. 5:8). Not that He had to learn to obey as we would say of a disobedient child, but rather in His capacity as man our great High Priest entered into every experience of the discipline of life. He who from all eternity had ruled and reigned over the far-flung universe which He had created and sustained by the word of His power yielded Himself to the discipline of experience, and in that way He learned obedience by the things which He suffered. For Him, the discipline of life as man involved among other things the fullest satanic temptations that were ever brought to bear upon a human being—the pain of being misunderstood by those who were nearest to Him by human ties, maligned falsely by the rulers, maliciously criticized by religious leaders, rejected and crucified by those whom He came to save. Nor was this mere chance or blind fate. It was by "the determinate counsel and foreknowledge of God" (Acts 2:23). Since this was the chosen pathway for the Son of God, dare we expect anything less than a life of discipline? He Himself said, "The disciple is not above his master, nor the servant above his lord. It is enough for, the disciple that he be as his master, and the servant as his lord" (Matt. 10:24-25).

The following Scriptures are in full accord with this:

John 16:33—"In the world ye shall have tribulation..."

James 1:12—"Blessed is the man that endureth
temptation: for when he is tried, he shall receive
the crown of life, . . ."
I Peter 1:7—". . . the trial of your faith, being
much more precious than of gold that perisheth,
though it be tried with fire, . . ."
I Peter 4:12—"Beloved, think it not strange concerning the fiery trial which is to try you, as though
some strange thing happened unto you."

These are only a few of the verses assuring us that
the godly must endure the discipline of life with its
attendant trials, which include sickness. Yet there is
a widespread belief among many sincere Christians
that ill health is never God's will for any of His children and that sickness should be considered a proof
that the sufferer is out of touch with God. Permit
a personal experience to illustrate this. At the age
of twenty years, the writer was stricken down with
pneumonia. The famous sulfa drugs were not then
available, and he lay in hospital for some weeks, very
near to the valley of the shadow. Much prayer was
made by the church; God graciously heard their
prayers and the dread crisis was safely passed. While
in this state of weakness, he had a visitor, a stranger
who came to the bedside and said, "Laddie, you are
very ill, but don't you know Jesus is the Healer?"
The writer answered, "Yes, I know Him; He is my
Saviour." To this she replied, "You know Him as
your Saviour, and that is wonderful, but why are
you not healed?" She then quoted Hebrews 6:6 and
said, "Laddie, by lying there on that bed of sickness,
don't you realize that you are crucifying the Son of
God afresh and putting Him to an open shame?"

Being too weak to argue, he had to lie and listen to the teaching that sickness was like sin and should have no place in the life of a Christian.

While admitting that sometimes sickness is a direct result of sin and often a punishment for sin, we dare not build a doctrine upon such a basis, and then make sweeping generalizations. Job's testings, including his broken health, were not the result of, nor a punishment for, sin in his life. On the contrary, he was subjected to such sufferings *because* of his unchallengeable sanctity. As we have seen, it was because Satan could not tempt him to commit known sin that he was taken through such deep trials. But far from separating him from God, Job's trials had the effect of bringing him into closer fellowship with God than he had ever known before.

3. *By trials, the saints are purified.* "Knowing this, that the trying of your faith *worketh* patience" (James 1:3-4). "We glory in tribulations also: knowing that tribulation *worketh* patience,..." (Rom. 5:3-5). "For our light affliction, which is but for a moment, *worketh* for us a far more exceeding and eternal weight of glory" (II Cor. 4:17). From these three passages of Scripture we who are the children of God learn that trials are not our masters to beat us down but should become our servants to "work" for us in producing that likeness to Christ which is the purpose of the whole plan of redemption. The writer of the Epistle to the Hebrews goes so far as to say that if we do not have the bitter experience of chastisement, then we are not truly the sons of God (Heb. 15:8).

4. *God does not promise to preserve us from trials.* Paul's experience is sufficient proof of this. He was

not delivered *from* his trial, but most certainly he was delivered *in* it. (II Cor. 12:7-10.) In that painful experience Paul rose to thrilling heights of victory, learning that the grace of God was sufficient for his deepest need. So true was this that he seemed to develop a new capacity for suffering as he enjoyed the fullness of satisfaction in the abundant grace of Christ, for he said it was his supreme desire "to know him,...and the fellowship of his sufferings" (Phil. 3:10). That supply of grace was adequate to enable him to say with assurance, "We are more than conquerors through him that loved us. For I am persuaded, that neither death, nor life, nor angels, nor principalities, nor powers, nor things present, nor things to come, nor height, nor depth, nor any other creature, shall be able to separate us from the love of God, which is in Christ Jesus our Lord" (Rom. 8:37-39). Thus we see that while we are not preserved from trials, we shall, if we yield to the Spirit of God, use them as stepping-stones to climb to new heights of fellowship with God. In this way the most bitter trial becomes a vehicle of eternal good to us.

5. *Such trials teach us that self must die.* The plain teaching of Paul in Romans, chapters 6 to 8, needs no comment here. It is not hard for the mind to understand this truth; the difficulty lies rather with the will, which to the last resists such a painful doctrine.

6. *Death to self was taught by our Lord Himself* (John 12:23-25). Only as the corn of wheat dies, does it really live. Our Lord Himself *must* die in order that eternal life, life more abundant, may forever flow. "And whosoever doth not bear his cross, and come after me, cannot be my disciple" (Luke

14:27). There is nothing sentimental about that phrase "bear his cross"! At the time when the Lord first used that figure of speech, every man who heard it knew that the cross was an instrument of death, painful death, and *only* death! Later centuries of Christian (or semi-pagan Christian) thought, made the cross an ornament to be worn on the body or portrayed in public places, but as the words fell from the lips of Christ, He intended all to understand that to be a disciple involved a death of the old nature, as complete and as painful as crucifixion. To be our Saviour, Jesus renounced all, and went to the Cross. To be His disciple, I renounce all, and take up the Cross. And yet modern Christianity holds out both hands for all the blessings which flow from His death, while the "flesh" stoutly refuses to die and accept the pathway of true discipleship.

Asceticism is not the answer! Vainly have men tried to evade the lusts of the "flesh" by ascetic practices. The hermits who sought to overcome the old nature by fasting and self-inflicted torture and complete isolation were in actual fact engaging in a form of occupation with the "flesh." But, as we have seen, the only means of overcoming the claims of the flesh is occupation with Christ.

As we consider Him, and meditate on the height and breadth and depth of His love and grace and holiness, we, like Job, are made to abhor the self-life in all its subtle manifestations, seeing in them the things that made the Cross of Calvary a bitter necessity for our Lord and Master.

When John of Patmos beheld the vision glorious of his risen and glorified Lord, he fell at His feet as *dead!* May we, like John, experience what it is to have our minds filled with the vision of Christ, the vision that casts the old nature into the dust as dead and enables the soul to enter into the fullness of life in the heavenlies with Christ!

If Job was indeed the first book of the Bible to be written, and since John's Revelation certainly is the last, we are left with the conclusion that from beginning to end, the Bible sets before us the doctrine of "death to self" as the answer to our deepest spiritual needs. "For this is the will of God, even your sanctification" (I Thess. 4:3).